Frederick A. McCord

Errors in Canadian History Culled from Prize Answers

Frederick A. McCord

Errors in Canadian History Culled from Prize Answers

ISBN/EAN: 9783337190163

Printed in Europe, USA, Canada, Australia, Japan

Cover: Foto ©Suzi / pixelio.de

More available books at **www.hansebooks.com**

ERRORS

IN

CANADIAN HISTORY

CULLED FROM

"PRIZE ANSWERS"

BY

FRED. A. McCORD

ONE OF THE COMPETITORS FOR THE SOLUTION OF THE
ONE HUNDRED QUESTIONS OF THE
" CANADIAN SPECTATO

MONTREAL
DAWSON BROTHERS, PUBLISHERS
1880

ERRATA.

Page 7, line 14, for 1661, read 1663.

" " 20, for 1662, read 1663.

" 31 " 21 " 1799 " 1797

" 42 " 14 " 1797 (July 12) read 1796

ERRORS

IN

CANADIAN HISTORY.

In the month of May, last year, the Canadian Spectator, of Montreal, began the publication, extending over several weeks, of one hundred Questions in Canadian History, and announced that several prizes would be given to those persons who, within a stated period, would furnish the greatest number of correct answers. The answers which were considered correct by the Spectator appeared in its columns in October and November, and some time in December the result of the competition was made known, and "Hermes," (Mr. Henry Miles, Jnr., of Montreal,) was declared to be the winner of the first prize.

Hermes has recently published his answers in pamphlet form, with the supposed weight attaching to the fact of his being the winner of the first prize ; and his answers are, in nearly every case, literally the same as those which the Spectator, with the assumed authority of a judge in the matter, decided to be the right ones.

Additional prestige arises from the fact that he is the son of a well-known writer of Canadian History, whose works are used as text-books in many of our schools ; and, moreover, the statement has been made in the public prints, and has not been contradicted, that the numerous notes and comments, forming part of the appendix, are from the pen of Mr. Miles' father. In these notes, only two or three of the answers are declared to be "not altogether faultless," and it may therefore fairly be inferred that, in the majority of instances, the assertions of Hermes have the sanction of his father's approval.

These circumstances are of a nature to induce the public to consider the information furnished by Hermes as particularly trustworthy, and to accept his evidence as decisive ; but it would be desirable to know whether this confidence is really well-founded, and whether the contents of the pamphlet in question are suited to be, according to the publisher's intention, "generally useful and interesting to those who may be in any way connected with the promotion and diffusion of the knowledge of our local history."

Now the truth is that not only are the answers given by Hermes not "correct in ninety-nine cases out of the hundred," but that, on the contrary, more than twenty of them are incorrect. Most of these are completely wrong ; a few are inexact as to dates and other particulars ; and in some instances, as will be shown, the answers given are either not borne out by, or in direct opposition to, the authorities cited in support of them.

That the Spectator's first prize should have been awarded to Hermes for a certain number of answers, many of which are incorrect, is of itself but a minor consideration : but that erroneous statements relating to the history of our country should not be widely circulated through the press, under the favouring circumstances just mentioned, without being controverted, is a matter of considerable importance, and has been deemed sufficient, in the opinion of the writer, to warrant the publication of the following pages, which, it is hoped, may prove both useful and welcome to students and all others who take an interest in Canadian History.

The errors which form the subjects of these notes are, for convenience sake, considered under separate headings, and in the order in which the answers they occur in were published.

EARLIEST MENTION OF LACROSSE.

Lacrosse, as at present played, is said to be of comparatively recent date, though in a simpler form it was a favourite pastime of the Indians centuries ago. The earliest mention of it which I have seen, occurs in Sagard's *Voyages au pays des Hurons*, published in Paris in 1632. From the ex-

pression made use of by Sagard (page 174), "*crosser
une balle de bois leger comme l'on faict en nos quartiers*,"
it would appear that it was not unlike some game
then played in France. But Hermes might seem
to have discovered a still earlier reference to the
game, for his answer, as to when it is first mentioned, is " 1608. Le jeu de crosse. Ferland's History of
Canada, vol. I, page 133." This was accepted by
the Spectator as correct. Upon referring to the
authority cited, I was astonished to find that page
133 forms part of a chapter on the Indians, their
customs, etc., and that " 1608 " is only a portion of
the running heading of that chapter, and by no
means intended for the date of the first mention
of any of the customs therein described. Besides,
Ferland could have given such an early date only
on authority other than his own, his history being
a recent publication. Hermes may perhaps be able
to account for this singular error.

FIRST MILITARY ORGANIZATION ON RECORD.

Question No. 21 was : " What is the oldest military organization of which there exists an authentic
record of formation," and Hermes states that it is
the celebrated Carignan Regiment, which was
disbanded in 1668, soon after its arrival in Canada.
He says : " Tracts of land were granted to its officers and men who chose to settle in the Colony,
and, in case of attack by the Iroquois or by the
Anglo-American colonists, they were expected,

from their former experience in warfare, to be able to immediately organize an adequate defence of the whole colony." This, I think, cannot be accepted as an answer to the question : for it is only said that they were expected to be able to organize and not that there was an actually existing organization.

According to Faillon, the military fraternity of " La Très-Sainte Vierge," composed of sixty-three men, was formed at Villemarie in 1653,—*Histoire de la Colonie Française*, vol. II, p. 213, and vol. III. p. 15, 3rd line ; and the " Militia of The Holy Family of Jesus, Mary, and Joseph," was formed, also at Villemarie, in 1661,—*Id.*vol. II, p. 16, and p. 20 note. These fraternities, therefore, and not the Carignan Regiment, seem to be " the first military organizations of which there is an authentic record of formation."

The *militia* of the Holy Family was formed in January 1662, and must not be confounded with the *confrérie* of the Holy Family which was formed in July of the same year.

THE " ROYAL WILLIAM."

It has been frequently asserted that the first vessel which crossed the Atlantic, *by steam-power alone*, was a Canadian-built steamer, the " Royal William." I do not now intend to discuss the question of Canada's right to this distinction, but

simply to note the inexactness of the following
answer given by Hermes to question 23 :—"The
Royal William sailed from Quebec 18 Aug. 1833,
touched at Pictou, N. S., and arrived at Gravesend
Sept. 11th, and was commanded by Captain Mc-
Donald." I am aware that the Canadian Antiquarian, (vol. IV, p. 79,) might be cited in corrobora-
tion of this statement ; but, as a matter of fact,
the Royal William left Quebec for London at 6 A.
M. on the 5th August, and not on the 18th which
was the date of her leaving Pictou. Further, the
Captain's name was not McDonald, but John Mc-
Dougall.—See *Christie's History of Canada*, vol. V, p.
362, and the *Quebec Gazette* of Aug. 5, 1833.

SLAVERY IN CANADA.

Slavery appears to have been introduced into
Canada about 1689, and its existence was recogni-
zed during more than a hundred years. The Spectator put the question (No. 27) : "When was the
last negro slave publicly sold in Montreal," and
Hermes answers that "the last slave publicly sold
in Montreal was in 1797. The deed was passed
by Mr. Gray and his partner, notaries. Manuel
was the name of the slave." This sale gave rise
to a lawsuit, the particulars of which, as well as
of the deed of sale, are related in the essay on slavery in Canada, published by *La Société Historique
de Montréal* in 1859 ; but I can find nothing
whatever to justify the assertion that it was a

— 9 —

public sale. I should say that the notaries themselves, Mr. Gray and his colleague, may have been *public*, but that the sale certainly was not.

CATHOLICS AND PROTESTANTS IN THE SAME CHURCH.

There are at least two instances on record of Catholics and Protestants having worshipped in the same church. The Protestants of Quebec were allowed the frequent use of the Recollet Church during several years previous to its destruction by fire on the 6th Sept. 1796 ; and in Montreal the same permission was granted them by the Recollets for some years, until the opening of the St. Gabriel Street Church in 1792.

" Long before, however," says Hermes, " de Caen *compelled* Roman Catholics and Protestants to worship *together* in the same Church at Quebec.—Recorded by Faillon, vol. I, p. 212, and cited by Leclercq, vol. I, pp. 332 and 341." The way in which the authorities are given would lead many to suppose that Faillon is first in point of time, and that he is cited by Leclercq, who, however, really lived two hundred years before him. But let that pass. Faillon does indeed state the facts as Hermes gives them, and cites the same pages of Leclercq ; but he is not borne out by his authority. Leclercq, after saying that De Caen wished to compel the French Catholics to attend the prayers of the Protestants, adds " *on n'en exécuta rien.*" Therefore

Catholics and Protestants did not then worship
in the same church. This occurs at page 333; but
Faillon commits the trifling error of citing page
332. As this slight inaccuracy is also committed,
or copied, by Hermes, I consider it pretty strong
evidence that he quotes Leclercq only at second
hand.

ANNEXATION.

The history of the Rebellion Losses Bill, the riots
which attended its passing, and the annexation
movement which took place in the same year, are
all well remembered facts. With reference to annexation, here is what Hermes says :—"In 1849,
after the sanction of the Rebellion Losses Bill, 350
persons, mostly of some local importance, at a tur-
bulent meeting on the Champ de Mars, Montreal,
signed a manifesto, declaring that annexation to
the United States was the only remedy for the
political and commercial condition of the country."
It is quite true that a meeting was held on the
Champ de Mars, on the evening of April 25, 1849,
after the passing of the Rebellion Losses Bill, and
immediately before the burning of the Parliament
House ; but I believe that no mention was there
made of annexation, and certainly no manifesto
was signed. At this meeting, it was simply resol-
ved that a committee be appointed to draft a petition to the Queen praying for Lord Elgin's recall,
and this petition was read at a meeting held at

the same place on the afternoon of the 27th. Shortly afterwards the British American League was formed in Montreal and in some cities of Upper Canada, with a view to changes in the Constitution and to consider the commercial state of the country. Its first meeting was held at Kingston, where, on the 31st July, it adopted an address to the people of Canada, setting forth the three prominent objects of the organization, as follows :—1° A Union of all the British American Provinces ; 2° Retrenchment and Economy in the public expenditure ; 3° Protection for Home Industry. But it was not till the early part of October that the Manifesto of the Annexation Association of Montreal, which had succeeded the League, was published in the newspapers. This was the first proposition of annexation in that year, and was made more than five months after the meeting on the Champ de Mars.

SETTLEMENT OF OTTAWA.

In any book which I have had an opportunity of consulting for a solution of the question : When and by whom was Bytown (now Ottawa) settled ? the one answer given is that " Bytown was founded in 1827 by Col. John By." This is part of the answer given by Hermes, who adds that Bytown " was settled by those engaged in the construction of the Rideau Canal." There is no very apparent reason for the date assigned, even supposing the

first settlement to have been made by Col. By.
He was sent out from England to superintend
the construction of the Rideau Canal, and on the
21st of Sept. 1826 the excavation for the locks
was commenced. This is therefore the true date
of the actual beginning of the canal, although the
first stone of the locks was not laid till the 16th of
Aug. 1827, by Captain (afterwards Sir John) Frank-
lin.

But the site of the present city of Ottawa was
not without an occupant when Col. By arrived,and
on this point I have received the following interesting personal reminiscences from a gentleman
still resident at Ottawa : " In 1817, Sergeant Berry
and his son-in-law Isaac Firth settled near where
the Chaudière bridges now are. They kept a
tavern. The next settlers, near the foot of the present timber-slide, were Hollister and Captain Col-
lins, and then Bellows and Stacy who built the
first stone house. These persons were all established and doing business before the survey of the
canal.—About the year 1818, a provincial land sur-
veyor, named John Burrows, owned the land, say
200 acres, on which the principal part of the city
of Ottawa now stands. Nicholas Sparks bought
from John Burrows about two years afterwards.
There was then built a log shanty, in which Mr.
Sparks lived for some years after he purchased the
property, and he was therefore the first settler in
that part of the city."

ST. HELEN'S ISLAND.

St. Helen's Island, opposite Montreal, was so
called by Champlain in honor of his wife, Hélène
Boullé, whose name is commonly, but incorrectly
spelled Bouillé. Hermes states that it was granted
to Charles LeMoyne on the 3rd of Nov. 1672.
A large grant of land was indeed made, on that
day, to Charles LeMoyne, father of the first Baron
de Longueuil ; but it did not include, either St.
Helen's Island or the small one next to it called
Ile Ronde. They had both been granted to Le
Moyne eight years previously, on the 30th of May,
1664, by de Lauzon Charny. I refer Hermes to
Faillon, vol. III, p. 350 note, or to the title (*titre*)
erecting the Barony of Longueuil, from which title
an extract is given in Appendix A.

CHAMPLAIN AND ST. LAWRENCE RAILROAD.

The name of the first Railway Company in Canada was "The Company of Proprietors of the
Champlain and St. Lawrence Rail-road." The
petition for incorporation was presented Nov. 23,
1831, and, notwithstanding the counter-petition
of the inhabitants of various parts of the Counties
of Chambly and Laprairie, who were in favour of
a turnpike road, a charter was obtained on the
25th Feby. 1832,—not, as stated by Hermes, in
1831. The Railway was to extend from Laprairie

to St. Johns, a distance of about sixteen miles, and work was begun in 1835. The road was opened for traffic in Aug. 1836, and was at first run with horses, but in 1837 locomotives were introduced in their stead.

LIEUT. COL. WINFIELD SCOTT.

Lieut Col. (afterwards General) Winfield Scott was taken prisoner at the battle of Queenston Heights, Oct. 13th 1812, and sent, with several others, to Quebec. During the ensuing winter he returned to the United States, and soon afterwards joined the army at Fort Niagara, as Lieutenant General to General Dearborn who was in chief command. By some it is said that he had been released on parole, which he would therefore have broken, while American writers assert that he had been duly exchanged in January 1813. This is a disputed point, and one which Hermes possibly places among "debatable questions," though he does not say so, but contents himself with mentioning that Scott was exchanged. It is, however, beyond doubt that he was paroled. The circumstances will be found stated at considerable length in the General Orders of Feb. 8, 1813.—See Appendix B.

OLDEST INCORPORATED TOWN IN ONTARIO.

I am particularly curious to know what authority Hermes has for considering Toronto the oldest incorporated town in Ontario. It was incorporated, as he says, in 1834,—but as a *city*,—and I am not aware of its having ever been an incorporated town. The town of Hamilton, incorporated in 1833, was, I believe, the first in Ontario.—See *Upper Canada Statutes.*

In a note to his answer, Hermes adds that "Kingston was incorporated in 1838, and Niagara in 1845." This may be intended as interesting information, but it seems somewhat strangely chosen ; for there where several incorporated towns in Upper Canada, before either Kingston or Niagara received its charter.—See Appendix C.

"LA MAISON MONTCALM."

The quaint little building, on the corner of St. Louis and Garden streets, opposite the St. Louis Hotel, is frequently spoken of as the oldest in Quebec, and there are good reasons for ascribing to it this superior antiquity, but they should at all events be correctly stated. Hermes says that the present owner "has in his possession a deed of *its* transfer on Nov. 30th 1674," and the obvious inference is of course that the house was previously

built. But this deed of Nov. 30, 1674, makes over
the land only on which the house now stands, and
contains a stipulation that it should be built upon
within a year from that date. Whether this condition was complied with, or not, I have been un-
able to ascertain.

OLDEST TOWN IN THE DOMINION.

Hermes declares that the oldest town in the Dominion is " Port Royal, now Annapolis, founded
1605.—Ferland vol. I, page 68, edition of 1861," and
he might wish to strengthen his position by pro-
ducing a score of other authorities on Canadian
History who readily admit that " Quebec is, next
to Annapolis, the oldest town in Canada."

I questioned the truth of this assumption, and,
after some research, arrived at the conclusion that
Quebec, and not Annapolis, is the oldest town in
the Dominion. This was my answer to the Spectator's question, and, although it was not accepted,
I still maintain its correctness, which I think is
easily proved.

Le Sieur de Monts, who had been appointed the
French King's Lieutenant General for Acadia,
came out in 1604 with several followers, among
whom was Champlain, and about a hundred colonists. After exploring a great part of the coast, he
settled at the mouth of the St. Croix river ; but
this place was found to be badly chosen. Half of

the colonists died from scurvy during the winter, and in the following spring De Monts removed to the shores of what is now called Annapolis Basin, and there formed a settlement which was named Port Royal. This was in 1605. A detailed narrative of the whole expedition was written by Champlain, who gives a carefully prepared map of Port Royal; and Marc Lescarbot, a Parisian lawyer, who arrived from France in the following year, has left an interesting account, which is also accompanied with maps. It is clearly shown on these maps, as well as by the text itself, that Port Royal was *on the north side* of Annapolis Basin, nearly opposite Goat Island. It was abandoned in 1607, re-occupied in 1610, and destroyed by the Virginians under Captain Argall in 1613. In 1620 it was re-settled by a number of Scotch colonists, and after the treaty of St. Germain, restored to the French, who almost immediately abandoned it; the fort was demolished; and the seat of government was removed for a time to La Hève, on the Atlantic coast of Nova Scotia, not far from the present seaport of Lunenburg. I meet with no mention of De Monts Port Royal subsequent to 1632.

Sometime between that year and 1645, a new settlement, also called Port Royal, was formed by d'Aulnay Charnisay, governor of Acadia, *on the south side* of Annapolis Basin, and a fort was built there, of which the ruins are still to be seen.—See Moreau, *Histoire de l'Acadie*, and *Winthrop's Journal*. It is this second Port Royal which was taken

2

erection : " for, as already stated, the present fort,
to which the question refers, was not built in
1665, but in 1711 ; it was never called Fort Char-
train, but Fort Pontchartrain ; and Captain de
Chambly did not superintend the erection of this,
but of the previous fort.

The "Old Fort at Chambly," the only relic of
the kind in North America, has long been deserted
and uncared for, and is fast crumbling away.

FIRST DISTILLERY.

It is claimed by Hermes that the first distillery
in Canada was erected by "the Hon. John Young
at Quebec, about the year 1788," and Bouchette's
Topography of Lower Canada (p. 422), is given as
authority. Now Bouchette places this distillery,
not at Quebec but at Beauport : "on the bank of
the River Beauport, are the distillery and mills
erected about twenty five years ago by the Honor-
able John Young at a very great expense ; they
are seated on the western bank of the river, over
which there is a bridge leading past them ; the
former belongs at present to Mr. Racy, the latter
to Mr. McCallum." Bouchette's *Topography* was
published in 1815.

Still the distillery at Beauport was not the first
at or near Quebec : there was one at Quebec several
years previously, and it is repeatedly mentioned
in the Journal of the Siege of 1775-6, kept by an
officer of the garrison.—See Appendix D.

This distillery was probably the first in Canada; but the question still remains,—When was it built ?

THE FIRST SCHOOLMASTER.

"When and where was the first Day School opened in Canada ? "—Hermes gives the following answer :—" In 1632, Rev. Father Le Jeune opened the first Canadian School at Quebec.—Relations des Jésuites, cited in Canadian Antiquarian, and in Dr Miles' School History of Canada, p. 59, and French Regime, p. 96."

In the *Relations des Jésuites*, it is stated that Father Paul Le Jeune opened a school for boys at Quebec, and that his scholars, from two in 1632, had increased to twenty in the following year ; and Dr Miles, at page 59 of his School History of Canada, remarks that " this worthy ecclesiastic has the honor of meriting the title of the *earliest schoolmaster in Canada.*"

I am sorry to have to deprive Father Le Jeune of that honour ; but the facts are clear. The Jesuits arrived in Canada in 1625 : the Recollets had come out with Champlain as early as 1615. Frère Pacifique Duplessis, in 1616, had a school for the Indians on the spot where Three Rivers was afterwards founded, and about the same time Father Joseph Le Caron opened a school at Tadousac. Hence it may with good reason be said that the

first teachers in Canada were the Recollets, Frère
Duplessis and Father Le Caron.—See Dr Meilleur's
Memorial de l'Education, Montreal, 1860.

SETTLEMENT OF LACHINE AND ORIGIN OF THE NAME.

Among the questions put by the Spectator was
this one,—No. 74 : " What is the date of the settlement of Lachine, and from what did it derive its
name ? "

It is usually said that in 1669 Dollier de Casson,
LaSalle and twenty others, started from here on
an exploring expedition, and that LaSalle and his
men having soon returned, notwithstanding their
boast that they were going to find a passage to
China, the place was derisively called La Chine.
This origin of the name has been questioned, but
it is probably correct.

As to the date of the settlement, Hermes informs
us that " Lachine began to be settled about the year
1678, when LaSalle established a post there ; but
the priests of the Seminary had a mission there and
held religious services ten years earlier."

Now LaSalle, in 1678, was still in France, where
he had gone three years before, and he did not
return to Quebec till the 15th Sept. He almost
immediately proceeded with a few followers to
Fort Frontenac, (now Kingston,) which had been
granted to him by the King, and he certainly cannot have been at Lachine during that year at least.

The real facts are as follows : Sometime between the autumn of 1667 and the autumn of 1668, Cavelier de LaSalle, then just arrived from France, received from the Sulpicians a gratuitous grant of a large tract of land about nine miles from Ville-marie. The precise date of the grant has not been ascertained. LaSalle appears to have at once commenced to clear the land, and before the end of the year 1668 he had disposed of portions of it to other settlers, and had begun the erection of buildings for his settlement, which he named St. Sulpice. The first settlement of Lachine, as this place was subsequently called, was therefore in 1667-8.—See Faillon, *Histoire de la Colonie Française*, vol. III, and the notes which accompany *Le Voyage de MM. Dollieret Galinée*, published by *La Société Historique de Montréal*, in 1875.

SUNDAY SCHOOLS.

With reference to the first establishment of Sunday Schools in Canada, the Spectator stated that " on Sept. 6th 1793, the *Quebec Gazette* announced the opening of the Sunday Free School under the patronage of H. R. H. the Duke of Kent ; but the lessons taught were reading, writing and arithmetic, and not of a religious character." Thereupon the following comment is made in the Appendix to Mr. Miles' pamphlet :—" The school opened by Prince Edward, at Quebec, on Sept. 4th 1793, can scarcely be styled a Sunday School in the sense in which the term is now employed. It was simply a *free school* in which *secular and elementary branches were taught on Sundays.*"

It is somewhat strange that the Spectator declined to accept the clear statements of the *Quebec Gazette*, with reference to Lord Dorchester's reception of Prince Edward, yet unhesitatingly admits the same paper as sufficient authority in the present instance, when it is not even correctly cited. The *Quebec Gazette* of the 5th Sept. 1793 does not say that a school of any description had been opened : it merely contains an advertisement announcing that it was intended to open a Sunday Free School on the 6th of October following. I have found no subsequent record on the subject in the colums of the Gazette.—See Appendix E.

Before discussing the question whether this school may be considered a Sunday School, according to any particular meaning of that expression, would it not be proper to ascertain what proofs there are that the school itself ever existed ?

STE. ANNE, BOUT DE L'ILE.

St. Ann's is about twenty miles from Montreal, and is a village of perhaps 1000 inhabitants. From its being situated on the south west end of the Island of Montreal, it is commonly called St. Ann's, Bout-de-l'Ile, to distinguish it from a dozen other St. Ann's in the Province of Quebec. Most persons imagine that it is a place of no consequence, noted at most as a summer resort for a few Montrealers, or as being mentioned in Tom Moore's Canadian Boat Song, and there was some surprise when the following appeared as the Spectator's 81st question : — " Give some remarkable events which occurred at St. Anne's, Bout-de-l'Ile."

The only well defined " event " which I could discover is this : " In 1776 a party of about 600 Americans under Arnold retired there, after being defeated near Vaudreuil by Captain Forster, who had only one-third the number of men and was encumbered with prisoners taken at the Cedars. Captain Forster proposed a *cartel*, which Arnold readily assenting to, on May 27th an exchange was effected for 2 majors, 9 captains, 20 subalterns, and 443 soldiers."—*Smith's History of Canada*, vol. II, p. 140.

But of what remarkable occurences does Hermes consider St. Ann's the scene ?—His answer is stated in his pamphlet in the following words :— " Thomas Moore wrote the Canadian Boat Song there in 1804.—" Dr. Scadding, &c."—Destruction of the Fort, &c.—A massacre by the Indians, Life of LeBer."

It is improbable that the answer was actually sent in this shape, and I think it may not unjustly be assumed that it was really the same as part of the answer which is given by the Spectator and which I now quote :—

" Thomas Moore is supposed to have written his well known Canadian Boat Song there in 1804."

" It is said that from the old fort situated there molten lead was poured upon the besiegers. The fort was burnt by the Iroquois in 1671, and by the Americans in 1812."

" Daulac or Dollard de Casson's [Dollard des Ormeaux is confounded with the Rev. Dollier de Casson] " fight with the Indians took place near there."

" Jeanne LeBer spent many years of self-imposed penance in a room in a tower which is still in existence."

The remainder of the answer is the event relating to Arnold, which I have already mentioned.

Did Tom Moore write the Canadian Boat Song at St. Ann's ?—Hermes appears to give Dr. Scadding, author of "Toronto of Old," as his authority for answering in the affirmative ; but I submit that Dr. Scadding is no authority on this point. The song is generally found with the heading, " Written on the River St. Lawrence," and in the early editions of Moore it is printed with a long explanatory note, part of which I subjoin :

" The above stanzas are supposed to be sung by those *royageurs* who go to the Grand Portage by the Utawas River.

" I wrote these words to an air which our boatmen sung to us very frequently. The wind was so unfavourable that they were obliged to row all the way, and we were five days in descending the river from Kingston to Montreal, exposed to an intense sun during the day, and at night forced to take shelter from the dews in any miserable hut upon the banks that would receive us.

"At the Rapid of St. Ann they are obliged to take out part, if not the whole, of their lading. It is from this spot the Canadians consider they take their departure, as it possesses the last church on the island, which is dedicated to the tutelar saint of voyagers."—(This paragraph is from Mackenzie's *General History of the Fur Trade*.)

Since Moore came down the St. Lawrence from Kingston to Montreal, and does not mention having gone out of his way to visit St. Ann's, there seems to be no reason to suppose that the Canadian Boat Song was written there.

The other events, supposed to have taken place at St. Ann's, Bout-de-l'Ile, are not of a nature to confer upon the spot very wide-spread celebrity, even if any of them had really occurred there, and not at another St. Ann's, to which the question does not refer. As to the case of Jeanne LeBer, it is the opinion of the Spectator and, presumably, of Hermes, that she " spent many years of self-imposed " penance in a room in a tower which is still in " existence ; " and that the tower is " still in exis-tence," is apparently added as evidence in favour of the truth of the story connected with it ; but it is about as conclusive as the well-known argu-ment of the author of " The Innocents Abroad " : " Such is the legend of the Seven Sleepers, and I know it is true because I have seen the cave myself."

Jeanne LeBer, the daughter of the richest merchant of Montreal, was born in 1662. She completed her education at the Ursulines Convent in Quebec about 1677, and then remained in her father's house, completely isolated from the outer world, till 1695. In that year she retired to the Convent of the Congregation nuns, and there, in a small room specially built for her at the back of the Chapel, passed the remaining nineteen years of her life in complete seclusion. The "many years of self-imposed penance" were therefore spent in Montreal, and not at St. Ann's where probably Mlle. LeBer never went. The Chapel was destroyed by fire in 1768, and the present Church of Notre-Dame de Pitié is the second which has since been erected on the same spot.—*Vie de Mlle. LeBer, Montreal*, 1860.

PROVINCIAL TROOPS WHICH TOOK PART IN THE CONQUEST OF CANADA.

Hermes does not furnish a very clear enumeration of the "Provincial" troops which took part in the conquest of Canada ; and his list of the battles in which they were engaged is neither complete, nor altogether correct, nor even quite in harmony with his enumeration of the forces. For instance, I find that he does not name the troops that took part in the capture of Fort Duquesne, though that is given by him as one of the battles ; and Pepperell's York Regiment, from Maine, could

scarcely have taken part in any of the battles
named, as it was disbanded in 1748.

It may be noted that the battle of Carillon was
fought on the 8th of July, and not on the 5th as
stated by Hermes and others.

No Provincial troops, except a few Rangers,
were present at the battle of the Plains of Abraham
or of St. Foy.

The following lists of troops and of battles have
been compiled from the New-York Colonial Documents and other authentic sources. The second
list still leaves a good deal to be desired; but
some one else may be able to supply the missing
names and form a perfect record.

Battles.

Monongahela.....................July   9, 1755
Lake George......... ....Sept. 8, "
Oswego...........................Aug. 11, 1756.
Sabbath Day Point...............July 26, 1757.
Fort George......................Aug. 9, "
Fall of Louisbourg...............June 26, 1758.
Carillon........... ....July 8, "
Fort Frontenac...................Aug. 25, "
Fort Duquesne......... ....Nov. 24, "
Ticonderoga......................July 22, 1759.
Fort Niagara......... ....   "   24, "
Beauport Flats...................   "   31, "
Plains of Abraham.. ....Sept. 13, "
St. Foy................ ....Apr. 28, 1760.
Surrender of Montreal..........Sept. 8, "

Provincial Troops.

The Provincial regiments were usually named
after their commanding officers, and those which

took part in the battles on the foregoing list were
as follows :

Connecticut :—	1st, or Lyman's.
	2nd, or Whitney's.
	Fitch's.
	Worster's.
Maine :—	Waldo's.
Massachusetts :—	1st, or Ruggles'.
	2nd, or Titcomb's.
	3rd, or William's.
	Bagley's.
	Partridge's.
	Preble's.
	Whitcomb's.
	Willard's.
New Hampshire :—	Blanchard's.
	Goffe's.
New Jersey :—	Johnston's.
	Parker's.
	Schuyler's.
New York :—	De Lancey's.
	Douty's.
	3rd, or Woodhull's.
	Johnson's.
Rhode Island :—	Babcock's.
	Harris'.

There were also several corps of Rangers, and,
at Fort Duquesne, troops from Carolina, Maryland,
Pennsylvania, and Virginia.

LIEUTENANT GOVERNORS OF QUEBEC.

Fifteen questions on difficult points of Canadian
history appeared in the *Quebec Morning Chronicle*
in June 1879, and two prizes were offered by Count

de Premio Real for the greatest number of correct
answers.

The prizes were awarded to Dr. N. E. Dionne, of
Quebec, who, although he has thrown no new light
on the subjects of the questions, has since published a pamphlet containing the result of his re-
searches, including his answer to this question :
" Give the names of all the Lieutenant Governors
of Quebec and Gaspe, from 1762 to 1838." He
gives the following list of Lieutenant Governors
of Quebec :

Sir Guy Carleton	1766	to 1768
Frederick Haldimand	1778	1785
Henry Hamilton	1785	1786
Henry Hope	1786	1786
Sir Alured Clarke	1791	1793
Sir Robert Shore Milnes	1799	1805
Sir Francis Nathaniel Burton	1824	1825

This answer is incorrect, inasmuch as it gives
the name of Frederick Haldimand, who was not
Lieutenant Governor but Governor in Chief, and
incomplete, because it makes no mention of Cramahé and Robert Prescott, who *were* Lieutenant
Governors. Besides, the dates given by Mr. Dionne
indicate the period during which these persons
administered the government, in the absence of
the Governor General, and do not indicate the period during which they held the position of Lieutenant Governors. The Lieutenant-Governorship
was perfectly distinct from the office of an administrator, and the two should not be confounded.

Guy Carleton's commission as Lieutenant Governor is dated April 7, 1766, and he would appear

to have held the office till Oct. 26, 1768, when he
was sworn in as " Captain General and Commander in Chief of the Province of Quebec."

The next Lieutenant Governor, of whom I find
any record, is Cramahé and not Haldimand. "On
Thursday last, the 17th instant, the members of the
Hon. the Legislative Council for this Province met
at the Castle of St. Louis in this City, in confor-
mity to the summons issued by His Excellency
the Governor for that purpose, when the King's
commission constituting and appointing the Hon.
Hector Theophilus Cramahé, Esq., Lieutenant
Governor of this Province, was read," etc.—*Quebec
Gazette,* Aug. 24, 1775.

Cramahé, having been transferred to the lieutenant-governorship of Detroit, was succeeded,
between 1780 and 1784, by Henry Hamilton, who
in turn was replaced by Henry Hope in 1785.

Hope died on the 13th April 1789, and was fol-
lowed by Lieutenant Governors Alured Clarke
(1790 to 1795), Robert Prescott (1796 to 1799), and
Robert Shore Milnes (1800 to 1807).

The last of these Lieutenant Governors of Quebec was Francis Nathaniel Burton, who was appointed Nov. 29, 1808, and held the sinecure till his
death at Bath, in England, on the 27th Jan. 1832.

In connection with this subject of Lieutenant
Governors, it has occurred to me that a list of the
French and English Governors of Canada may
prove acceptable, and in the appendix to these
notes will be found one which I had compiled for

my own use. I have endeavored to make it more
detailed and accurate than any which I have yet
seen, and the dates are in every instance derived
from trustworthy sources, such as the *Relations*
and *Journal* of the Jesuits, the *New York Colonial
Documents*, the *Quebec Gazette* and *Mercury*, and the
Official Gazette.

In the list of French Governors there are several
dates wanting ; but it is nevertheless published
without these, in the hope that other friends of
Canadian History may be able to complete it.

With reference to the English Governors, it
should be noted that although Amherst is usually
placed first on the list, it is well known that after
the capitulation of Montreal he divided the province into three governments or districts, to each
of which he appointed a Governor, and that he
himself very shortly afterwards left the country
and did not return. The Governors of these three
districts, during what is commonly called the
period of military rule, from Sep. 8, 1760, to Aug.
10 1764, were as follows :—

District of Quebec,
    Gen. James Murray...Sep. 1760 to Aug. 1764.
District of Three Rivers,
    Col. Ralph Burton.....Sep. 1760 to May 1762.
    Col. Fred. Haldimand.May 1762 to Mar. 1763.
    Col. Ralph Burton.....Mar. 1763 to Oct. 1763.
    Col. Fred. Haldimand.Oct. 1763 to Aug. 1764.
District of Montreal,
    Gen. Thomas Gage.....Sep. 1760 to Oct. 1763.
    Col. Ralph Burton.....Oct. 1763 to Aug. 1764.

APPENDIX A.

Extract from title (titre) erecting the Barony of Longueuil, dated at Ville-Marie 10th July 1676.

" Est comparu pardevant nous," Duchesneau, the Intendant " Charles Lemoyne, Ecuyer, sieur de Longueuil, lequel nous a remontré qu'il est en possession d'une terre en fief et seigneurie appellée Longueuil, sictuée en la cote 'du sud sur le bord du grand fleuve St. Laurent, vis-à-vis de cette ville de Ville-Marie, contenant deux lieues ou environ de terre de front, tenant d'un costé aux terres du Sr. de Varennes, et d'autre à celles de la seigneurie de la Prairie de la Magdelaine, laquelle lui a esté donnée et concédée avec l'Isle appellée Ste. Hélène, et l'islet rond et autres isles, islets et bastures adjacentes de la dite seigneurie, sçavoir : par le Sr. de Lauzon de la Citière, le nombre de cinquante arpens de terre de front sur cent de profondeur, en fief et seigneurie, avec tous droits de haute, moyenne et basse justice, à la charge de la foy et hommage,... par titre en date du vingt-quatrième septembre mil-six-cent-cinquante-sept ; par le sieur de Lauzon Charny, les dites isles de Ste. Hélène et islet rond, par billet de luy signé, en date du trentième may mil-six-cent-soixante-et-quatre, aux charges qu'il plairoit au sieur de Lauzon y apposer, ensuite de quoy le dit sieur de Lauzon comme tuteur, et ayant la garde noble des enfans mineurs de feu sieur de Lauzon, grand sénéchal de ce pays,

3

auquel appartenoit la seigneurie de la Citière,
auroit donné et concédé au dit sieur Lemoyne les
dites isles de Ste. Hélène et islet rond, pour par
luy en jouir en fief,... par titre datté à Paris le
vingtième mars mil-six-cent-soixante-et-cinq, signé
de Lauzon, et contresigné Jeanville."

APPENDIX B.

GENERAL ORDERS.

ADJUTANT GENERAL'S OFFICE,

QUEBEC, 8TH FEBRUARY 1813.

HIS EXCELLENCY LIEUT. GENERAL SIR GEORGE
PREVOST, Bart. Governor in Chief and Commander
of the Forces in British North America, having
seen in the Boston Gazette of the 28th January
last, a publication purporting to be a copy of a
General Order issued by the American Government, in the following terms, namely :

" Adjutant General's Office,"

" Washington City, 18th Jan. 1813."

" General Orders."

" The following Officers of the Army and Militia of the United States, made prisoners of War at
Detroit, Queenston and elsewhere, have been duly
exchanged for the Officers, non-commissioned Officers, Drummers and Privates, taken on board his

Britannic Majesty's Transport Samuel and Sarah, on the 11th day of July 1812, *viz.* Brigadier General William Hull, Colonel Duncan McArthur, James Fundly, and Lewis Cass; Lieutenant Colonels James Miller, John R. Fenwick, Winfield Scott, and John Christie; Major James Taylor; Captain Nathan Heald, John Whistler, Henry B. Brevoort, Josiah Snelling, Robert Lucas, Abraham F. Hull, Peter Ogilvie, William King, Joel Cook, and Return B. Brown; First Lieutenant Charles Larrabe; Second Lieutenants James Dalliba and Daniel Hugunin: And each and all of the aforesaid officers are hereby declared exchanged, and as free to act against the united Kingdom of Great Britain and Ireland, and the dependencies thereof, as if they had never been captured."

" By order of the Secretary of War."

" T. H. Cushing. Adjutant Genl."

His Excellency considers himself called upon in the most public manner, to protest against the pretended release of the above named Officers from their Parole of Honor, given under their hands while Prisoners of War. His Excellency having expressly refused to accede to the exchange of the officers above named, as proposed to him by Major General Dearborn in his Letter of the 26th Dec. and 2d. Jan. last under the authority of the American Government, upon the identical terms contained in the Order of the 18th of January before referred to, His Excellency feels himself compelled hereby to declare, that he still considers those officers as

Prisoners of War, on their Parole, and that should the fate of war again place any of them at the disposal of the British Government, before a regular and ratified Exchange of them takes place, they will be deemed to have broken their Parole, and to be thereby subject to all the consequences sanctioned by the established usage of War in the like cases.

The detachment of the 1st Regiment, or Royal Scots captured by the U. S. frigate the Essex, on board the Samuel and Sarah Transport, who are stated in the said Order of the 18th of January to have been duly exchanged for the officers of the American Army therein mentioned, had been previously, as far back as the month of September last, regularly exchanged for the Crew of the U. S. Sloop Nautilus, and a sufficient number of other Seamen belonging to the U. S. Navy, as appears by an official communication to His Excellency of the 7th of September last, from His Excellency Lieut. Genl. Sir J. C. Sherbrooke, K. B., commanding the forces in Nova Scotia, confirmed by a Letter from Mr. Mitchell, the American Agent of Prisoners at Halifax, to the Honble James Monroe, American Secretary of State, dated the 23rd of November last, transmitted to His Excellency by Major Genl. Dearborn, in his Letter of the 2d of January last. The release of the said detachment by such Exchange, was published in General Orders on the 29th September last, at Montreal, and also communicated to Major Genl. Dearborn, in His Excellency's Letter of the 11th of January

last, as the ground of his refusal to accede to the
before mentioned proposal of that Officer.

....

ADWD. BAYNES,
Adj. Genl. North America.

APPENDIX C.

Incorporated Towns in Ontario down to 1845.

Hamilton,	3 Wm. IV, ch. 17	Feb. 13, 1833.
Toronto. (City)	4 Wm. IV, " 23	Mar. 6. 1834.
Belleville,	" " 24	" "
Cornwall,	" " 25	" "
Port Hope,	" " 26	" "
Prescott,	" " 27	" "
Cobourg,	7 Wm. IV, ch. 42	Mar. 4, 1837.
Picton,	" " 44	" "
Kingston,	1 Victoria, " 27	Mar. 6, 1838,
London,	3 " " 31	Feb. 10, 1840.
Niagara,	8 " " 62	Mar. 29, 1845.
St. Catherines,	8 " " 63	" "

APPENDIX D.

Extracts from a "Journal of the most remarkable occurrences in Quebec, from the 14th of November 1775, to the 7th of May 1776. By an Officer of the Garrison."

Jany 22, 1776.—Wind N. E. drifty, cloudy, not
cold. About two this morning some houses in St.

Roe were set on fire. A quantity of rum and molasses has lain in Mr. Drummond's distillery until now ; part of it was got in to-day--the fire may spread that way.

Jany 24.—Mild fine weather, wind S. W. Firing at the guard-hcuse in St. Roe. Rum and molasses brought into town.

March 1.—Cold N. W. wind. The voluntary picquet very strong last night. Some people seen on the other side St. Charles river, opposite to Mr. Drummond's distillery ; we fired the 24 pounder behind the Hotel Dieu at them. About seven o'clock in the evening, a house under that gun was perceived to be on fire in the roof; it burnt in a short time to the ground ; some think that the wadding fell on the roof; others imagine the rebels may have set it on fire, in hopes that the flames would spread to the distillery, from thence to the picquets above, and so to Montcalm's house, from thence the conflagration would become general."

APPENDIX E.

From the Quebec Gazette of Thursday, 5th Sept. 1793.

From an ardent desire of promoting the happiness and prosperity of his Majesty's faithful subjects of this Province, and from the experience of the many and great advantages that have been received from the Sunday Schools in England, under the patronage of the Nobility and Royal Family ; his Royal Highness PRINCE EDWARD has been pleased strongly to recommend to the Subscriber to open a Sunday Free School for the benefit of all those of every description, who are desirous of acquiring the necessary and useful Branches of Education, and will conform to the Rules and Regulations that will be made for that purpose.

The said Free School will therefore be opened the first Sunday in the next month, under the Patronage and Directions of his Royal Highness, from the hours of ten to three during the Winter season. And the Public may depend on every exertion on the part of the Subscriber, in order to meet in every respect his Royal Highnesses benevolent intentions.

The Subscriber requests those who wish to attend to give him their names as soon as possible. He may be seen every day from nine to twelve, and from two to five at the Academy in the Bishop's Palace, where young people of both sexes will be taught in separate apartments all the various Branches of Literature, on terms most suitable to their circumstances.

JAS. TANSWELL

Quebec, 5th Sept. 1793.

FRENCH GOVERNORS OF CANADA.

	DATE OF COMMISSION.	FROM.	TO.
CHAMPLAIN, Samuel de....................	Oct. 15, 1612	Oct. 15, 1612	July 20, 1629
CHAMPLAIN, Samuel de....................	—	May 23, 1633	Dec. 25, 1635
CHATEAUFORT, Marc Antoine Bras-de-fer de (a)...	—	Dec. 25, 1635	June 11, 1636
MONTMAGNY, Charles Huault de........	—	June 12, 1636	Aug. 19, 1648
D'AILLEBOUST de Coulonge, Louis........	—	Aug. 20, 1648	Oct. 12, 1651
LAUZON, Jean de........................	Jan. 17, 1651	Oct. 13, 1651	— 1656
LAUZON-CHARNY, Charles de............	—	— 1656	Sep. 12, 1657
D'AILLEBOUST de Coulonge, Louis........	—	Sep. 13, 1657	July 10, 1658
D'ARGENSON, Pierre de Voyer, Vicomte...	Jan. 26, 1657	July 11, 1658	Aug. 30, 1661
D'AVAUGOUR, Pierre Dubois, Baron......	—	Aug. 31, 1661	July 23, 1663
MEZY, Augustin de Saffray..............	May 1, 1663	Sep. 15, 1663	May 5, 1665
COURCELLES, Daniel de Rémy de (b)......	Mar 23, 1665	Sep. 12, 1665	— 1672
FRONTENAC, Louis de Buade, Comte de Palluau et de...	Apr. 7, 1672	Sep. — 1672	— 1682
LA BARRE, Le Fèbvre de (c)..............	May 1, 1682	Oct. 9, 1682	— 1685
DENONVILLE, Jacques René de Brisay, Marquis de...	Jan. 1, 1685	July — 1685	Oct. 11, 1689

FRONTENAC, Louis de Buade, Comte de Palluau et de............	May 15, 1689	Oct. 15, 1689	Nov. 28, 1698
CALLIERES, Louis Hector de............	—	Nov. 29, 1698	Sep. 13, 1699
CALLIERES, Louis Hector de (e)............	Apr. 20, 1699	Sep. 14, 1699	May 26, 1703
VAUDREUIL, Philippe de Rigaud, Marquis de............	—	May 27, 1703	Sep. 16, 1705
VAUDREUIL, Philippe de Rigaud, Marquis de (e)............	Aug. 1, 1703	Sep. 17, 1705	Oct. 10, 1725
RAMSAY, Claude de............	—	— 1714	— 1706
LONGUEUIL, Charles LeMoyne, (1st.) Baron de............	—	— 1725	— 1726
BEAUHARNOIS, Charles, Marquis de (e)............	Jan. 11, 1726	Sep. 2, 1726	— 1747
LA GALISSONNIÈRE, Rolland Michel Barrin, Comte de............	June 10, 1747	Sep. 19, 1747	Aug. 14, 1749
LA JONQUIÈRE, Jacques Pierre de Taffanel, Marquis de............	Mar. 15, 1746	Aug. 15, 1749	May 17, 1752
LONGUEUIL, Charles LeMoyne, (2nd.) Baron de............	Mar. 1, 1752	May — 1752	July — 1752
DUQUESNE-De Menneville, Marquis de............	July — 1755	July — 1752	— 1755
VAUDREUIL-CAVAGNAL, Pierre de Rigaud, Marquis de............	Jan. 1, 1755	June 25, 1755	Sep. 8, 1760

Names in small capitals are those of administrators.

(a) The date given in the second column is that of Champlain's death. Chateaufort's administration began on the day of the interment, probably the 28th.

(b) The Marquis de Tracy, the King's *Lieutenant-General* in America, arrived at Quebec, June 30, 1665, and was virtually the Governor of Canada till his departure, Aug. 28, 1667.

(c) The date here given in the second column is that of the registration of the Governor's commission at Quebec.

ENGLISH GOVERNORS.

	FROM.	TO.	REMARKS.
			Names in small capitals are those of Administrators.
AMHERST, General Jeffrey (a)	Sep. 8, 1760	— —	
MURRAY, General James	Aug. 10, 1764	June 28, 1766	
IRVING, Paulus Æmilius	June 30, 1766	Sept. 23, 1766	a. The facts mentioned on page 32 will be sufficient to account for there being no date in the second column.
CARLETON, Lt. Gov. Guy	Sep. 24, 1766	Oct. 25, 1768	
CARLETON, Guy (b)	Oct. 26, 1768	June 26, 1778	
CRAMAHÉ, Hon. Hector Theophilus	Aug. 9, 1770	Oct. 10, 1774	
HALDIMAND, Frederick	June 27, 1778	Nov. 15, 1784	
HAMILTON, Lt. Gov. Henry	Nov. 16, 1784	Nov. 1, 1785	
HOPE, Lt. Gov. Henry	Nov. 2, 1785	Oct. 22, 1786	b. Guy Carleton was made a Knight of the Bath on the 6th of July, 1776.
DORCHESTER, Baron (c)	Oct. 23, 1786	July 11, 1796	
CLARKE, Lt. Gov. Alured	Aug. 17, 1791	Sep. 24, 1793	
PRESCOTT, Lt. Gov. Robert	July 12, 1797	Apr. 26, 1797	
PRESCOTT, Robert	Apr. 27, 1797	July 30, 1799	c. Sir Guy Carleton was named Lord Dorchester, on the 21st of August 1786.
MILNES, Lt. Gov. Robert Shore	July 31, 1799	July 30, 1805	
DUNN, Hon. Thomas	July 31, 1805	Oct. 23, 1807	

CRAIG, Sir James Henry	Oct. 24, 1807	June 19, 1811
DUNN, Hon. Thomas	June 20, 1811	Sep. 13, 1811
PREVOST, Sir George	Sep. 14, 1811	July 15, 1812
PREVOST, Sir George	July 16, 1812	April 4, 1815
DRUMMOND, Sir Gordon	April 5, 1815	May 21, 1816
WILSON, Major Gen. John	May 22, 1816	July 11, 1816
SHERBROOKE, Sir John Coape (d)	July 12, 1816	July 29, 1818
RICHMOND, Charles, Duke of	July 30, 1818	Aug. 28, 1819
MONK, Hon. James	Sep. 20, 1819	Feb. 7, 1820
MAITLAND, Sir Peregrine (e)	Feb. 8, 1820	Feb. 8, 1820
MONK, Hon. James	Feb. 9, 1820	Mar. 16, 1820
MAITLAND, Sir Peregrine	Mar. 17, 1820	June 18, 1820
DALHOUSIE, George, Earl of	June 19, 1820	Sep. 7, 1828
BURTON, Lt. Gov. Sir Francis Nathaniel (f)	June 7, 1824	Sep. 16, 1825
KEMPT, Sir James	Sep. 8, 1828	Oct. 19, 1830
AYLMER, Matthew Whitworth Aylmer, Baron	Oct. 20, 1830	Feb. 3, 1831
AYLMER, Matthew Whitworth Aylmer, Baron	Feb. 4, 1831	Aug. 23, 1835
GOSFORD, Archibald Acheson, Earl of	Aug. 24, 1835	Feb. 26, 1838
COLBORNE, Sir John	Feb. 27, 1838	May 28, 1838
DURHAM, John George Lambton, Earl of	May 29, 1838	Oct. 31, 1838

d. On the 12th of July, 1816, Sir John Sherbrooke took the oaths of office at Quebec, although he had previously, on the 8th of June, been sworn in at Halifax.

e. Sir Peregrine Maitland, Governor of Upper Canada, was sworn in at Quebec, as Administrator of the government of Lower Canada, on the 8th of February. He returned to Upper Canada next day; but came back to Quebec in March, and was again sworn in on the 17th.— Quebec Mercury.

f. Sir Francis Nathaniel Burton was the last of the Lieutenant Governors of Quebec.

COLBORNE, Sir John	Nov. 1, 1838	Jan. 16, 1839
COLBORNE, Sir John	Jan. 17, 1839	Oct. 18, 1839
SYDENHAM, Chs. Ed. Poulett Thomson, Lord, (g)	Oct. 18, 1839	Sep. 19, 1841
Clitherow, Major Gen. John (h)	Sep. 18, 1841	Sep. 19, 1841
JACKSON, Sir Richard Downes	Sep. 24, 1841	Jan. 11, 1842
BAGOT, Sir Charles	Jan. 12, 1842	Mar. 29, 1843
METCALFE, Sir Charles Theophilus (i)	Mar. 30, 1843	Nov. 25, 1845
CATHCART, Charles Murray, Earl of	Nov. 26, 1845	Apr. 23, 1846
CATHCART, Charles Murray, Earl of	Apr. 24, 1846	Jan. 29, 1847
ELGIN, James Bruce, Earl of	Jan. 30, 1847	Dec. 18, 1854
Rowan, Major Gen. William (h)	May 29, 1849	May 30, 1849
ROWAN, Lieut. Gen. William	Aug. 23, 1853	June 10, 1854
HEAD, Sir Edmund Walker	Dec. 19, 1854	Oct. 24, 1861
EYRE, Sir William	June 21, 1857	Nov. 2, 1857
WILLIAMS, Sir William Fenwick	Oct. 12, 1860	Feb. 22, 1861
MONCK, Charles Stanley, Viscount	Oct. 25, 1861	Nov. 27, 1861
MONCK, Charles Stanley Viscount (j)	Nov. 28, 1861	Nov. 13, 1868
MICHEL, Sir John	Sep. 30, 1865	Feb. 12, 1866
WINDHAM, Sir Charles Ashe	Nov. 14, 1868	Nov. 30, 1868
YOUNG, Sir John	Dec. 1, 1868	Feb. 1, 1869

g. The Hon. C. Poulett Thompson was created Baron Sydenham and Toronto in 1840. The date given in the first column is that of his assuming the Governorship of Lower Canada, of which province he was the last Governor. He was sworn in as Governor of the Province of Canada, on the 10th of February, 1841, when Upper and Lower Canada were united.

h. Acted merely as Deputy of the Governor for the prorogation of parliament. The name is retained because it appears on other lists.

i. Sir Charles Metcalfe was created Baron Metcalfe in January, 1845.

j. Lord Monck was Governor of the Province of Canada until the first of July, 1867. On that day, the Dominion of Canada was proclaimed, and he was sworn in as the first Governor.

			k. Sir John Young was elevated to the peerage, with the title of Lord Lisgar, on the 8th of October, 1870.
YOUNG, Sir John (k.................	Feb. 2, 1869	June 21, 1872	
DOYLE, Sir Charles Hastings............	June 22, 1872	June 24, 1872	
DUFFERIN, Sir F. T. H.Blackwood, Earl of.....	June 25, 1872	Oct. 18, 1878	
O'GRADY HALY, Lieut. Gen. William........	Oct. 12, 1874	Nov. 2, 1874	
O'GRADY HALY, Lieut. Gen. William........	May 15, 1875	Oct. 22, 1875	
O'GRADY HALY, Gen. Sir William........	Jan. 21, 1878	Feb. 6, 1878	
MACDOUGALL, Sir Patrick Leirne	Oct. 19, 1878	Nov. 24, 1878	
LORNE, Sir John D. S. Campbell, Marquis of.......	Nov. 25, 1878	———	

www.ingramcontent.com/pod-product-compliance
Lightning Source LLC
Chambersburg PA
CBHW021548270326
41930CB00008B/1409